A Day in Japan

Daniel Moreton • Samantha Berger

Scholastic Inc.
New York • Toronto • London • Auckland • Sydney

Acknowledgments
Literacy Specialist: Linda Cornwell
Social Studies Consultant: Barbara Schubert, Ph.D.

Design: Silver Editions
Photo Research: Silver Editions
Endnotes: Jacqueline Smith
Endnote Illustrations: Anthony Carnabucia

Photographs: Cover: Diana Walker/Gamma Liaison; p. 1: Collins/The Image Works; p. 2: Diana Walker/Gamma Liaison; p. 3: Paul Chesley/Tony Stone Images; p. 4: J. Nordell/The Image Works; p. 5: Cameramann/The Image Works; pp. 6–7: Alan Levenson/Tony Stone Images; p. 8: Fujifotos/The Image Works; pp. 9, 10: Charles Gupton/Tony Stone Images; p. 11: Charles Gupton/The Stock Market; p.12: Joseph Sohm/The Stock Market.

No part of this publication may be reproduced in whole or in part, or stored in a retrieval system, or transmitted in any form or by any means, electronic, mechanical, photocopying, recording, or otherwise, without written permission of the publisher. For information regarding permission, write to Scholastic Inc., 555 Broadway, New York, NY 10012.

Library of Congress Cataloging-in-Publication Data
Moreton, Daniel.
A day in Japan / Daniel Moreton, Samantha Berger.
p. cm. -- (Social studies emergent readers)
Summary: Simple text and photographs present children engaged in various activities in school, after school, and at home.
ISBN 0-439-04571-1 (pbk.: alk. paper)
1. Japan--Social life and customs--1945- --Pictorial works--Juvenile literature.
[1. Japan--Social life and customs.] I. Berger, Samantha. II. Title.
DS822.5.M63 1999

952.04--dc21

98-52726
CIP AC

Copyright © 1999 by Scholastic Inc.
Illustrations copyright © 1999 by Scholastic Inc.
All rights reserved. Published by Scholastic Inc.
Printed in the U.S.A.

12 13 14 15 16 17 18 19 20   08   6 7 8 9/0

Spend the day with us in Japan.

We wear uniforms to school.

We wear hats to school.

We take off our shoes at school.

We learn at school.

We eat lunch at school.

We play music after school.

We play baseball after school.

We eat dinner at home.

We read together at home.

Japan.

A Day in Japan

Children in Japan have a busy day. They go to school from 8:30 until 3:30 Monday to Friday, and even attend a shorter school day on Saturday. Most children are also involved in extracurricular activities at their schools. There's lots of homework to be done after school. Then there's dinner and time with the family, and of course, Japanese children love to play during the day, too!

Going to school Many Japanese schoolchildren wear a uniform. Sometimes girls wear blue sailor suits. Often they wear black or navy blazers, matching skirts, and a tie or ribbon. Boys also wear black or blue jackets with matching pants.

Japanese schoolchildren wear brightly colored hats to school. In a small school, all the children in the same grade wear the same color hat. In a larger school, each grade is broken up into different groups, and each group wears a different color hat. The hats make it easy for a child to find his or her group and for teachers to keep track of the children.

In school Japanese children leave their shoes at the entrance of their school. Japanese people often sit on the floor, on straw mats called tatami, or on large cushions. It is customary to leave shoes outside to avoid getting the mats or cushions dirty.

Reading and writing Japanese children spend a lot of time in school learning to read and write. Japanese is a very difficult writing system to learn. Japanese children have to memorize and learn to write kanji, a kind of writing in which each symbol means a whole word, and kana, another kind of writing that uses symbols for parts of words. In addition, Japanese children have to learn to read and write Roman script (that's the alphabet we use). Japanese students also study arithmetic, science, music, social studies, physical education, and home economics, as well as English. Art is important, too, including the Japanese art of calligraphy, which the boy in the picture is practicing. *Calligraphy* means "beautiful writing." The calligrapher uses a brush and ink to make beautiful "pictures" with words.

Lunch A healthy lunch is prepared for the students in the classroom each day. The students take turns serving. Usually there is a stew or curry made with some kind of meat or fish, boiled vegetables, a sandwich, and salad. Students drink milk with lunch. Dessert is usually ice cream or fruit.

After school After school many Japanese children play music. Some Japanese children start to play an instrument at a very young age—even two years old—using miniature instruments and without learning to read music. Other children play baseball after school. Little League baseball started in Japan in 1964. The 1,500 teams play in championships on the regional, national, and international levels.

At home Some Japanese families sit on chairs around a table to eat dinner. But in many Japanese homes today, families still follow the old tradition of sitting on cushions on the floor around a low table. Japanese cooking is very healthy. Japanese people eat lots of fresh fish and vegetables, often raw. There is rice and green tea with every meal. The Japanese eat with chopsticks and sometimes forks.

After dinner many families take some time to read with their children. It's nice to spend time together, especially for the father, who usually works very long hours six days a week. Many mothers do not work outside the home. Their main responsibilities are the home and the children, especially the children's education. In fact, some mothers are so involved with trying to help their children do well in school that they have a nickname, "education Moms." Reading together in the evening is not only fun, but it is also a good opportunity for parents to give their children more practice with written Japanese. Japan has one of the highest literacy rates in the world.

Flag The Japanese flag has a red circle on a white background. The circle represents the sun. In the past Japanese people believed that their emperor was a descendant of the sun goddess. The word *Japan* means "Land of the Rising Sun" in Japanese. The white part of the flag stands for purity and integrity. The red part stands for sincerity, brightness, and warmth.